THE Holiday
JOKE BOOK

What travels all over the world
but stays in a corner?
A postage stamp.

What has a trunk and holds 350 people?
A jumbo jet.

What does Rupert take on holiday?
All the bear essentials!

If you like holidays, you'll love
The Holiday Joke Book . . .

KATIE WALES

THE
HOLIDAY
JOKE BOOK

Illustrated by Mark Burgess

A Magnet Book

For Tim

First published as a Magnet paperback original 1987
by Methuen Children's Books Ltd
11 New Fetter Lane, London EC4P 4EE
Text copyright © 1987 Katie Wales
Illustrations copyright © 1987 Mark Burgess
Printed in Great Britain

ISBN 0 416 05392 0

Off We Go . . .

Knock, knock.
Who's there?
Holly.
Holly who?
Holidays are here again . . .

Why did the boy take an axe to school?
Because it was breaking-up time.

What is grey, has four legs and a trunk?
A mouse going on holiday.

What's green, has two legs and a trunk?
A sea-sick tourist.

Why do elephants have trunks?
*If they didn't, they wouldn't be able
to go swimming.*

Why else?
They'd look silly with suitcases, wouldn't they?

Who takes less time to pack for his holiday,
an elephant or a cockerel?
A cockerel: he only has to take his comb.

Did you hear about the elephant who took
two trunks on holiday – *one to drink with, and
one for swimming.*

What does Rupert take on holiday?
All the bear essentials.

What travels all over the world,
but stays in a corner?
A postage stamp.

Where do cows go for their holiday?
Moo York. (I bet you said 'Cowes'!)

Where do cats go for their holidays?
The Canary Islands.

How do you make a meat loaf?
Send it on holiday.

Have you heard about the kangaroo who crossed the Channel by hoppercraft?!

What skim across the Channel barking at cats?
Hovercrufts.

What's made of plastic and sails the Atlantic in five days?
A dustbin liner.

What do you get if you cross the Atlantic in the *Titanic*?
Halfway.

How do rabbits travel?
By hareplane.

What has a trunk and holds 350 people?
A jumbo jet.

Why don't elephants like flying?
Because their trunks won't fit under the seats.

Why aren't doctors travel-sick?
Because they're accustomed to see sickness.

What flies and wobbles?
A jellycopter.

What would happen if pigs could fly?
Bacon would go up.

What kind of fish do they serve on aeroplanes?
Flying fish.

Why did the elephant book two seats on the coach?
So the person next to him wouldn't get squashed.

Do you know that if you cross a jumbo jet with a kangaroo, you get a plane that makes short hops?

How do you get a mouse to fly?
Buy it an airline ticket.

When are you glad to be down and out?
After a bumpy flight.

Did you know that a witch's favourite holiday is witch-hiking?

What's a twip?
A wide in a twain.

What train has no wheels?
A train of thought.

Travellers' Tales . . .

Why is a guide-book like a pair of handcuffs?
It's for tourists (two wrists, geddit?).

What runs around Paris in a plastic
bag at noon?
The lunch-pack of Notre Dame.

Knock, knock.
Who's there?
Frances.
Frances who?
Frances capital is Paris.

What cereal do you get for breakfast in a
French hotel?
Huit heures bix.

What do you see from the top of the
Eiffel Tower?
An eyeful . . .

How do you address a drunken Roman?
'Hi! Tiddly Iti!'

What's purple and 3,000 miles long?
The grape wall of China.

What language do monkeys speak?
Chimpanese.

What speaks all languages?
An echo.

What is tall, made of dough and tilts?
The leaning Tower of Pizza.

What people travel the most?
Romans.

What makes the Tower of Pisa lean?
It never eats.

How do you make a Swiss roll?
Throw him off the top of the Alps.

What kind of birds are found in Portugal?
Portugeese.

How do you enter an Egyptian house?
Toot-and-come-in.

What do you call the little rivers that
flow into the Nile?
Juveniles.

Has your father ever gone on
overland expeditions?
Not safaris I know.

What is big, white and furry and is
found in Manchester?
A lost polar bear.

What's 3,000 miles long and breaks easily?
The Great Wall of China.

Where are the Andes?
At the end of the wristies.

What language is quack-quack?
Double ducks.

'Dad, I don't want to go to Australia
for my holidays.'
'Shut up and keep digging.'

'Mum, I don't want to go to Majorca
for my holidays.'
'Shut up, and keep swimming.'

What is the best thing to take to the Sahara
desert?
A thirst-aid kit.

What has two humps and is found
at the North Pole?
A lost camel.

Why wouldn't a traveller feel hungry in the
desert?
Because of the sandwiches there.

What kind of car do they drive in China?
A Rolls Rice.

What did Dracula visit in New York?
The Vampire State Building.

Sun Sizzlers . . .

What likes to spend summer in a fur coat?
A moth.

What's green, hairy and wears sun-glasses?
A gooseberry on holiday.

Did you hear about the elephant who wore
sun-glasses?
*He didn't want to be recognized because of all the
elephant jokes around.*

What is red and grey and hates to be touched?
A sunburnt elephant.

What is black and white and red all over?
A sunburnt penguin.

What letters are best read in the sun?
Fan mail.

What do bees say in the summer?
'Swarm'.

What do you get if you leave
bones in the sun?
A skeletan.

Why do bananas use suntan lotion?
Because they peel easily.

Seaside Sauce . . .

What is Noddy's favourite resort?
Redcar.

Why is the Isle of Wight a fraud?
*Because you can't milk the Cowes,
or thread the Needles.*

What is a witch's favourite seaside resort?
Sand-witch.

Why is there no honey in Brighton?
Because there's only one B in it.

Where is Felixstowe?
On Felix's foot.

What happens when you throw an
elephant into the sea?
He gets wet.

Why can't two elephants go
swimming together?
They only have one pair of trunks between them.

Why don't elephants like swimming?
Because they can't keep up their trunks.

What did the Martian say when he
landed at Brighton?
'Take me to your Lido.'

Why do elephants wear sandals?
To stop their feet sinking into the sand.

Why do ostriches bury their
heads in the sand?
To see the elephants who aren't wearing sandals.

Why do elephants swim upside down?
So they don't tread on the fish.

What goes in pink and comes out blue?
A swimmer on a cold day.

Where do ghosts like to swim?
Lake Eerie and the Dead Sea.

Why did Wally have trouble water-skiing?
He was looking for a sloping lake.

Why did Wally have trouble surf-riding?
He couldn't get his horse in the water.

What do you get if you cross an elephant with a goldfish?
Swimming trunks.

What do you get if you cross an
elephant with a whale?
Outsize swimming trunks.

Why is the sand wet?
Because the seaweed.

What did the beach say when
the tide came in?
'Long time no sea.'

What does the sea say to the beach?
Nothing, it just waves.

Why won't the sea fall into space?
Because it's tide.

What did the boat say to the pier?
'What's up, dock?'

What's the noblest part of the sea-side?
The pier.

How does a boat show affection?
It hugs the shore.

What do you get if you cross the
sea with a computer?
Brain-waves.

What children live by the sea-side?
Buoys and gulls.

Why was the crab arrested?
Because it kept pinching things.

What do you call a holidaymaker
with a seagull on his head?
Cliff.

Why did the lobster blush?
Because it saw the salad dressing.

What instrument does a
lighthouse-keeper play?
A fog-horn.

Who is the biggest gangster in the sea?
Al Caprawn.

What did one rock-pool say to the other?
'Show us your mussels.'

Why is the sea restless?
It has so many rocks in its bed.

What ices do monsters prefer?
I screams for help.

What do you get if you cross a
football team with ice cream?
Aston Vanilla.

What is little and pink and lives
in the rocks and sings?
Frankie Prawn.

What's black and zooms under
the sea at 500 mph?
A guided mussel.

Did you hear the one about the ghosts who
like to ride at the fairground – they go
on the Roller Ghoster.

What's green and goes 'putt, putt'?
An outboard pickle.

Ocean Antics

Can you cut the sea in half?
Yes, with a sea-saw.

What kind of oven does the ocean like to use?
A micro-wave.

Why couldn't the sailors play cards?
The Captain was standing on the deck.

How does a ship hear?
Through its engineers.

What geometric figure do sailors fear?
The Bermuda triangle.

Why is the sea always suspicious?
Because it's crossed so often.

Who was the first under-water spy?
James Pond.

What lies at the bottom of the sea and shivers?
A nervous wreck.

Who is always being let down by his mates?
A deep-sea diver.

Where is the sea deepest?
On the bottom.

What comes up from the bottom of the sea
and shouts 'Knickers'?
Crude oil.

What comes up from the bottom of the sea
and whispers 'Panties'?
Refined oil.

What does a deaf fish need?
A herring-aid.

What did one herring say to the other?
'Am I my brother's kipper?'

Did you know that fish learn
to swim in a school!

What's wobbly and lives in the sea?
A jelly-fish.

What fish do dogs chase?
Catfish.

Which fish terrifies the others most?
Jack the Kipper.

What fish is famous?
A star-fish.

How do you catch an electric eel?
With a lightning-rod.

Have you heard the joke about the eel? You
wouldn't grasp it.

What is the fishes' favourite TV programme?
'Name That Tuna.'

What fish make good shoes?
Soles and eels.

What happens to a fish when it feels dizzy?
Its head swims.

What is the most musical fish?
A piano tuna.

Why did the fish cross the ocean?
To get to the other tide.

Where are whales weighed?
At a whale-weigh station.

What do whales like to chew?
Blubber-gum.

How do you get two whales in a Mini?
Drive down the M4 . . .

Why do fish dislike Coca-Cola so much?
Because it's the reel thing.

What is the fastest fish?
A motor-pike.

What fish can't swim?
A dead one.

How can you get in touch with a fish?
Drop it a line.

What do you get if you cross a
shark and a helicopter?
A heli-chopper.

Who sailed the seas looking for rubbish and
blubber?
Binbag the whaler.

What is the noblest creature in the ocean?
The Prince of Whales.

What's a howling baby whale called?
A little blubber.

What else?
A little squirt.

What is a mermaid?
A deep-she fish.

What do sea-monsters eat?
Fish and ships.

What eats its victims two by two?
Noah's shark.

What's a shark's favourite hobby?
Anything it can get its teeth into.

What cat lives in the ocean?
An octopuss.

What lives in the ocean, has eight legs and is quick on the draw?
Billy the Squid.

Have you heard the one about the octopus who sang, 'I wanna hold your hand, hand, hand, hand, hand, hand, hand, hand . . .

What would you get if you crossed an octopus with a mink?
A fur coat with eight sleeves.

How does an octopus go into battle?
Well-armed.

What moves under the sea and
carries 64 people?
An octobus.

What does an octopus wear?
A coat of arms.

Why did the turtle cross the road?
To get to the Shell station.

What do rich turtles wear?
People-neck sweaters.

Country Corn . . .

What's the difference between a country
yokel and Welsh rarebit?
One's easy to cheat, and the others' cheesy to eat.

A lost tourist stopped and asked the
country yokel, 'Will this path take me
to the main road?'
   'No,' was the reply, 'You'll have
to go yourself.'

Another lost tourist asked the country yokel, 'Is this the right road for Shakespeare's birthplace?'

'Yes,' the man replied, 'But there's no hurry – he's dead.'

Why did the weeping willow weep?
Because it saw the pine tree pine.

Why did the snowdrop?
Because it saw the cro-cuss . . .

If a buttercup is yellow, what colour is a hiccup?
Burple.

Do rabbits have combs?
No, hare brushes.

If we get honey from bees, what do we get from wasps?
Waspberry jam.

Why did the cowslip?
Because it saw the bulrush.

Why is a rabbit's nose never shiny?
*Because she keeps her powder puff at
the other end.*

What would you get if you crossed a rabbit
with a watering-can?
Hare spray.

What do you get if you pour boiling water
down a rabbit-hole?
Hot cross bunnies.

What did the bee say to the flower?
'Hello, honey.'

What did the bee say to the rose?
'Hiya, bud.'

Why do bees hum?
Because they don't know the words.

What is worse than being with a fool?
Fooling with a bee.

What do bees do with all their honey?
They cell it.

Why did the bees go on strike?
For more honey and shorter flowers.

What do bees chew?
Bumble-gum.

What goes 'Zzub zzub'?
A bee flying backwards.

What kind of bee drops things?
A fumble bee.

What do you call a modest bee?
A humble bee.

What do you call a hesitant bee?
A maybee.

What do you call a little bee?
A babee.

What is a bee's favourite song?
'Comb Sweet Comb.'

Why is a bee's hair sticky?
Because it uses a honeycomb.

How does a bee get to work?
By buzz.

A hedgehog was fighting a fox: who won?
The hedgehog won, on points.

Why did the hedgehog cross the road?
To see his flatmate.

What goes dot-dot-croack, croak-croak-dot?
Morse toad.

Why did the otter cross the road?
To get to the otter side.

How do hedgehogs kiss each other?
With difficulty.

What did the mother hedgehog say to the
baby hedgehog before she spanked him?
'This will hurt me as much as it will you.'

How can you tell the difference between a
weasel and a stoat?
*A weasel's weasily identified, and a stoat's
stoatally different.*

What travels at 50 mph underground?
A mole on a motor-bike.

Where do frogs sit?
On toadstools.

Where do tadpoles change into frogs?
In the croakroom.

What are frogs' favourite stories?
Croak-and-dagger tales.

What kind of shoes do frogs wear?
Open toad ones.

What is a frog's favourite food?
Croak-ettes.

**What do you get if you cross
a frog and a dog?**
A croaker spaniel.

What games do frogs like to play?
Hop-scotch; and croak-et.

What do frogs drink?
Croaka-cola.

How do frogs and rabbits make beer?
With hops.

What is small and green and
says 'cloak, cloak'?
A Chinese frog.

What do you say to a hitch-hiking toad?
'Hop in.'

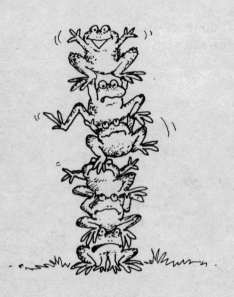

What do you call a lot of toads
on top on one another?
A toadem pole.

What is green and makes a loud noise?
A frog-horn.

How did the frog die?
It just croaked.

What is the best way to catch a squirrel?
*Hang upside-down from a tree and look
like a nut.*

What did one squirrel say to the other?
'I'm nuts about you.'

How do we know owls have short memories?
They keep saying 'Who? Who?'

Why did the owl make everyone laugh?
Because he was a hoot.

Why do birds in their nest agree?
Because they don't want to fall out.

What do you get if you cross a squirrel
with a kangaroo?
An animal that keeps its nuts in its pockets.

What did the beaver say to the tree?
'It's been nice gnawing you.'

What is black, lives in trees,
and is very dangerous?
A crow with a machine-gun.

What did the tree say to the beaver?
'Leaf me alone.'

Farmyard Fun . . .

What's small and green and loves camping?
A Boy Sprout.

Why was the farmer cross?
Someone had trodden on his corn.

Did you hear about the farmer who bought
100 battery hens, but they all died? He had
trouble putting the batteries in . . .

What did the blackbird say to the scarecrow?
'I'll knock the stuffing out of you.'

Why is a farmer like a magician?
Because he can turn a cow into a field.

Two farmers were discussing their cows.
'Rosie's got distemper,' said Fred. 'What did
you give your cow when she had it?'
'Turpentine,' said the other.
   A week later they met again at market. 'I
gave Rosie turpentine just like you said, and it
killed her,' complained Fred. 'Mine did too,'
said the other.

What is the difference between a farmer
and a dress-maker?
*One gathers what he sows, and the other sews
what she gathers.*

What happened when the farmer
fell down a well?
He kicked the bucket.

What do you get if you cross a cow
with a lot of money?
Rich milk.

What do you call a sleeping heifer?
A bull-dozer.

What do you call a cow that can't give milk?
An udder failure.

Did you hear about the scarecrow who was so scary the blackbirds brought back the seed they'd taken the week before . . .

What happens if you walk under a cow?
You get a pat on the head.

Did you hear about the cornfield where the corn was 50 feet high? A tall story . . .

Why shouldn't you gossip in a cornfield?
Because corn has ears, and beanstalk.

Why do cows wear bells?
Because their horns don't work.

What do you get if you cross a cow
with a camel?
Lumpy milkshakes.

Where do you find ancient cows?
In a moo-seum.

What do you call a cow that eats grass?
A lawn-mooer.

What do you get if you cross a cow
with an octopus?
An animal that can milk itself.

What is the difference between a sick cow
and an angry crowd?
One moos badly, the other boos madly.

When is the best time to milk a cow?
When she's in the moo-d.

How did the silly shepherd count his sheep?
Counted all their legs and divided by four.

How can you milk a mouse?
You can't, the bucket won't fit under it.

Why do white sheep eat more
than black ones?
Because there are more of them.

What did the ram say to his girl-friend?
'I love ewe.'

What do you get if you cross a sheep
with a rain-shower?
A wet blanket.

What do you get if you cross a sheep
with a porcupine?
An animal that knits its own sweaters.

Where does a sheep get its fleece cut?
At the baaber's.

Why are sheep like pubs?
Because they are full of baas.

What do lady sheep wear?
Ewe-niforms.

What do you call sheep who
write to each other?
Pen-pals.

Why did the sheep bump into the hedge?
He didn't see the ewe-turn.

What kind of warmth do sheep
have in the winter?
Central bleating.

What do you get if you cross a
sheepdog with jelly?
The collie-wobbles.

What do you get if you cross a sheepdog with
a bunch of buttercups?
Collieflowers.

What do you call a female goat?
A buttress.

What did the billy-goat say when he reached
the last thistle in the field?
'Thistle have to do.'

Why can't you trust fishermen and shepherds?
They both live by hook and by crook.

What do you get if you cross a
pig with an elephant?
Extra large pork chops.

What do you get if you cross a
pig with a zebra?
Striped sausages.

What do you get if you cross a pig with a flea?
Pork scratchings.

How do you get a pig to hospital?
By hambulance.

What do you call someone who steals pigs?
A hamburglar.

Where do pigs keep their money?
In a people-bank.

How does a pig write letters?
With pen and oink.

What does a pig use for medication?
Oinkment.

Why is the letter K like a pig's tail?
They both come at the end of pork.

How do chickens dance?
Chick-to-chick.

What is a hen's favourite vegetable?
An egg-plant.

Why did the hen sit on the axe?
So she could hatch-et.

How do we know that owls are
cleverer than chickens?
Have you ever heard of Kentucky Fried Owl?

What did the little chick say as it
came out of its shell?
'What an eggs-perience!'

What do you get if you cross a cockerel
with a wolf?
A bird that howls when the sun rises.

Where does a baby goose come from?
A gooseberry bush.

What runs round a field but never moves?
A hedge.

What is green and goes 'Boing, boing'?
Spring cabbage.

What else?
Spring onion.

What do you get if you cross
a duck with a cow?
Queam Quackers.

Why do ducks have webbed feet?
To stamp out forest fires.

What time do ducks get up?
At the quack of dawn.

What did the duck say when he
flew upside down?
'I'm quacking up.'

What do you call two rows of cabbages?
A dual cabbage-way.

What is green and goes 'Ooh-la-la'?
A French bean.

What vegetables fight crime?
Beetman and Radish.

What vegetable plays snooker?
A cue-cumber.

What game do horses like?
Stable tennis.

Why is a fox like a carpenter?
He can make a chicken run.

Zany Zoos . . .

How do zoo animals greet each other?
'Hi, Ena; Ello, Phant.'

What do they scrawl on the walls of zoos?
Giraffiti.

What is the snootiest animal in the zoo?
The giraffe – because it looks down on you.

What has a long neck and smells nice?
A giraffe-o-dil.

What is worse than a giraffe
with a sore throat?
An elephant with a nose bleed.

What is worse than that?
A turtle with claustrophobia.

What is worse than that?
A centipede with athlete's foot or fallen arches.

What is worse than that?
A snake with sore ribs.

Why did the dolphin-trainer prefer happy
dolphins?
Because he didn't like talking at cross porpoises.

Why don't elephants like Penguins?
They can't get the paper off.

What do you get if you cross a kangaroo
with a polar bear?
A fur coat with pockets.

Why does a polar bear have a fur coat?
Because he'd look silly in a plastic mac.

What do you get if you cross
a hyena and a cat?
A giggle puss.

What do you get if you cross
a hyena and a parrot?
An animal that laughs at its own jokes.

What do you get if you cross a lion
and a parrot?
I don't know, but if it wants a grape,
you'd better give it one.

What's the biggest mouse in the zoo?
A hippopotamouse.

What weighs a ton, likes mud, and goes up
the front of your anorak?
A zipperpotamus.

What weighs a ton, likes mud, and waves a
flower in the air, singing 'Peace'?
A hippy potamus.

What's black and white and noisy?
A zebra with a set of drums.

What's the difference between an
elephant and a rhino?
The elephant has a longer memory.

What's the difference between an elephant
and a bison?
You can't wash your hands in an elephant.

A little girl, on her first visit to the zoo, was
intrigued by the elephants. 'Look, Mummy,'
she exclaimed, 'they're picking up peanuts
with their vacuum cleaners!'

Why couldn't the leopard escape from the
zoo?
Because it was always spotted.

Is it hard to spot a leopard in the zoo?
No, it comes that way.

Holidays' End . . .

What did the hotel manager say to the
elephant who couldn't pay his bill?
'Pack your trunk and clear out!'

What dance do you do when the
holidays are over?
Tan-go.